Anonymous

The Soldier's Hymn-Book

For Camp Worship

Anonymous

The Soldier's Hymn-Book
For Camp Worship

ISBN/EAN: 9783337136765

Printed in Europe, USA, Canada, Australia, Japan

Cover: Foto ©ninafisch / pixelio.de

More available books at **www.hansebooks.com**

THE

SOLDIER'S HYMN-BOOK:

FOR

CAMP WORSHIP.

SOLDIERS' TRACT SOCIEY

Virginia Conference, M. E. Church,

1862.

CHAS. H. WYNNE, PRINTER.

HYMNS.

1

S. M.

Psalm xcv.

COME, sound his praise abroad,
  And hymns of glory sing;
Jehovah is the sovereign God,
  The universal King.

2 He form'd the deeps unknown:
  He gave the seas their bound:
The watery worlds are all his own,
  And all the solid ground.

3 Come, worship at his throne:
  Come, bow before the Lord:
We are his work, and not our own,
  He form'd us by his word

4 To-day attend his voice,
  Nor dare provoke his rod;
Come, like the people of his choice,
  And own your gracious God.

2

L. M.

Psalm c.

BEFORE Jehovah's awful throne
  Ye nations bow with sacred joy:
Know that the Lord is God alone,
  He can create, and he destroy.

2 Could my tears forever flow,
Could my zeal no languor know,
These for sin could not atone;
Thou must save, and thou alone;
In my hand no price I bring,
Simply to thy cross I cling.

3 While I draw this fleeting breath,
When my eyes shall close in death,
When I rise to worlds unknown,
And behold thee on thy throne,
Rock of ages, cleft for me,
Let me hide myself in thee.

6   ## C. M.

Resurrection of Christ.

THE Lord of Sabbath let us praise,
   In concert with the blest,
Who, joyful, in harmonious lays,
   Employ an endless rest.

2 Thus, Lord, while we remember thee,
   We bless'd and pious grow;
By hymns of praise we learn to be
   Triumphant here below.

4 On this glad day a brighter scene
   Of glory was display'd,
By God, th' eternal Word, than when
   This universe was made.

4 He rises, who mankind has bought
   With grief and pain extreme;
'Twas great to speak the world from naught;
   'Twas greater to redeem.

7

C. M.

Heb. iv. 14–16.

WITH joy we meditate the grace
    Of our High Priest above;
His heart is made of tenderness,
    His bowels melt with love.

2 Touch'd with a sympathy within,
    He knows our feeble frame;
He knows what sore temptations mean,
    For he has felt the same.

3 He in the days of feeble flesh
    Pour'd out strong cries and tears,
And in his measure feels afresh
    What every member bears.

4 He'll never quench the smoking flax,
    But raise it to a flame;
The bruised reed he never breaks,
    Nor scorns the meanest name.

5 Then let our humble faith address
    His mercy and his power:
We shall obtain deliv'ring grace
    In the distressing hour.

8

C. M.

Coronation of Christ.

ALL hail the power of Jesus' name!
    Let angels prostrate fall;
Bring forth the royal diadem,
    And crown him Lord of all.

2 Ye chosen seed of Israel's race,—
  A remnant weak and small,—
Hail him, who saves you by his grace,
  And crown him Lord of all.

3 Ye Gentile sinners, ne'er forget
  The wormwood and the gall :
Go, spread your trophies at his feet,
  And crown him Lord of all.

4 Let every kindred, every tribe,
  On this terrestrial ball,
To him all majesty ascribe,
  And crown him Lord of all.

5 O that, with yonder sacred throng,
  We at his feet may fall!
We'll join the everlasting song,
  And crown him Lord of all.

9   L. M.

Dying, rising, reigning.

HE dies! the Friend of sinners dies!
  Lo! Salem's daughters weep around;
A solemn darkness veils the skies;
  A sudden trembling shakes the ground:
Come, saints, and drop a tear or two
  For Him who groan'd beneath your load;
He shed a thousand drops for you,
  A thousand drops of richer blood.

2 Here's love and grief beyond degree,
  The Lord of glory dies for man !
But, lo! what sudden joys we see!
  Jesus, the dead, revives again!

The rising God forsakes the tomb;
 Up to his Father's courts he flies;
Cherubic legions guard him home,
 And shout him welcome to the skies!

3 Break off your tears, ye saints, and tell
 How high your great Deliv'rer reigns!
Sing how he spoil'd the hosts of hell,
 And led the monster death in chains!
Say, "Live for ever, wond'rous King!
 Born to redeem, and strong to save!"
Then ask the monster, "Where's thy sing?"
 And, "Where's thy vict'ry, boasting grave?"

10   C. M.

Rev. v. 11–13.

COME, let us join our cheerful songs
 With angels round the throne;
Ten thousand thousand are their tongues;
 But all their joys are one.

2 Worthy the Lamb that died, they cry,
 To be exalted thus:
Worthy the Lamb, our hearts reply,
 For he was slain for us.

3 Jesus is worthy to receive
 Honor and power divine;
And blessings more than we can give,
 Be, Lord, for ever thine.

4 The whole creation join in one.
 To bless the sacred name
Of Him that sits upon the throne,
 And to adore the Lamb.

11 **C. M.**

Salvation.

SALVATION, O the joyful sound!
  'Tis pleasure to our ears;
A sov'reign balm for ev'ry wound,
  A cordial for our fears.

2 Buried in sorrow and in sin,
  At hell's dark door we lay;
But we'll arise by grace divine
  To see a heavenly day.

3 Salvation! let the echo fly.
  The spacious earth around,
While all the armies of the sky
  Conspire to raise the sound.

12 **C. M.**

Stupendous love.

PLUNGED in a gulf of dark despair,
  We wretched sinners lay,
Without one cheering beam of hope,
  Or spark of glimm'ring day.

2 With pitying eyes the Prince of grace
  Beheld our helpless grief;
He saw, and (O amazing love!)
  He ran to our relief.

3 Down from the shining seats above
  With joyful haste he fled,
Enter'd the grave in mortal flesh,
  And dwelt among the dead.

4 O for this love let rocks and hills
   Their lasting silence break!
And all harmonious human tongues
   The Saviour's praises speak.

5 Angels, assist our mighty joys,
   Strike all your harps of gold;
But when you raise your highest notes,
   His love can ne'er be told!

13   C. M.

" He is precious."

JESUS, I love thy charming name,
   'Tis music to my ear;
Fain would I sound it out so loud,
   That earth and heaven should hear.

2 Yes, thou art precious to my soul,
   My transport and my trust;
Jewels, to thee, are gaudy toys,
   And gold is sordid dust.

3 All my capacious powers can wish,
   In thee doth richly meet;
Not to mine eyes is light so dear,
   Nor friendship half so sweet.

4 Thy grace still dwells upon my heart,
   And sheds its fragrance there;
The noblest balm of all its wounds,
   The cordial of its care.

5 I'll speak the honors of thy name
   With my last, lab'ring breath;
Then speechless clasp thee in my arms,
   The antidote of death.

C. M.

Witness and Seal of the Spirit.

WHY should the children of a King
  Go mourning all their days?
Great Comforter, descend, and bring
  The tokens of thy grace.

2 Dost thou not dwell in all thy saints,
  And seal the heirs of heaven?
When wilt thou banish my complaints,
  And show my sins forgiven?

3 Assure my conscience of her part
  In the Redeemer's blood;
And bear thy witness with my heart,
  That I am born of God.

4 Thou art the earnest of his love,
  The pledge of joys to come;
May thy bless'd wings, celestial Dove,
  Safely convey me home!

15   C. M.

The Spirit's quickenings implored.

COME, Holy Spirit, heavenly Dove,
  With all thy quick'ning powers,
Kindle a flame of sacred love
  In these cold hearts of ours.

2 Look how we grovel here below,
  Fond of these earthly toys;
Our souls, how heavily they go,
  To reach eternal joys!

3 In vain we tune our formal songs,
  In vain we strive to rise;
Hosannas languish on our tongues,
  And our devotion dies,

4 And shall we then forever live,
  At this poor dying rate?
Our love so faint, so cold to thee,
  And thine to us so great?

5 Come, Holy Spirit, heavenly Dove,
  With all thy quick'ning powers;
Come, shed abroad a Saviour's love,
  And that shall kindle ours.

16   C. M.

Lord's Day.

COME, let us join with one accord
  In hymns around the throne!
This is the day our rising Lord
  Hath made and call'd his own.

2 This is the day which God has blest,
  The brightest of the seven,
Type of that everlasting rest
  The saints enjoy in heaven.

3 Then let us in his name sing on,
  And hasten to that day
When our Redeemer shall come down,
  And shadows pass away.

4 Not one, but all our days below,
  Let us in hymns employ;
And in our Lord rejoicing, go
  To his eternal joy.

17

Holy Ghost invoked.

CELESTIAL Dove, Come from above,
   And guide me in thy ways;
My heart prepare, For solemn prayer,
   And tune my lips to praise.

2 Open mine eyes, And make me wise,
   My interest to discern;
From every sin, Without, within,
   Incline my heart to turn.

3 Fly to my aid, When I'm afraid,
   Or plunged in deep distress;
My foes subdue, And bring me through
   This howling wilderness.

18

S. M.

Lord's Day.

WELCOME, sweet day of rest,
   That saw the Lord arise:
Welcome to this reviving breast,
   And these rejoicing eyes!

2 The King himself comes near,
   And feasts his saints to-day;
Here we may sit, and see him here,
   And love, and praise, and pray.

3 One day within the place
   Which thou dost, Lord, frequent,
In sweeter than ten thousand days
   In sinful pleasures spent.

4 My willing soul would stay
    In such a frame as this,
And sit and sing herself away
    To everlasting bliss.

19   C. M.

Courage.

A M I a soldier of the cross,—
    A foll'wer of the Lamb,—
And shall I fear to own his cause,
    Or blush to speak his name?

2 Must I be carried to the skies
    On flowery beds of ease,
While others fought to win the prize,
    And sail'd through bloody seas?

3 Are there no foes for me to face?
    Must I not stem the flood?
Is this vile world a friend to grace
    To help me on to God?

4 Sure I must fight if I would reign;
    Increase my courage, Lord;
I'll bear the toil, endure the pain,
    Supported by thy word.

5 Thy saints, in all this glorious war,
    Shall conquer, though they die;
They see the triumph from afar,
    By faith they bring it nigh.

6 When that illustrious day shall rise,
    And all thy armies shine,
In robes of vict'ry, through the skies,
    The glory shall be thine.

Four 6s and two 8s.

The year of Jubilee.

BLOW ye the trumpet blow,
The gladly solemn sound;
Let all the nations know,
   To earth's remotest bound,
The year of jubilee is come;
Return, ye ransom'd sinners, home.

2 Jesus, our great High Priest,
   Hath full atonement made:
Ye weary spirits, rest;
   Ye mournful souls, be glad:
The year of jubilee is come:
Return, ye ransom'd sinners home.

3 Extol the Lamb of God,
   The all-atoning Lamb;
Redemption through his blood
   Throughout the world proclaim;
The year of jubilee is come;
Return, ye ransom'd sinners, home.

4 Ye slaves of sin and hell,
   Your liberty receive,
And safe in Jesus dwell,
   And bless'd in Jesus live:
The year of Jubilee is come;
Return, ye ransom'd sinners, home.

5 Ye who have sold for naught
   Your heritage above,
Receive it back unbought,
   The gift of Jesus' love:
The year of jubilee is come;
Return, ye ransom'd sinners, home.

6 The gospel trumpet hear,
    The news of heavenly grace;
And, saved from earth, appear
    Before your Saviour's face;
The year of jubilee is come;
Return, ye ransom'd sinners, home.

21   **7s.**

The Expostulation.

SINNERS, turn, why will ye die?
    God, your Maker, asks you why!
God, who did your being give,
Made you with himself to live,—
He the fatal cause demands,
Asks the works of his own hands,
Why, ye thankless creatures, why
Will ye cross his love, and die?

2 Sinners, turn, why will ye die?
God, your Saviour, asks you why!
Christ, who did your souls retrieve,
Died himself that ye might live:
Will ye let him die in vain?
Crucify your Lord again?
Why, ye ransom'd sinners, why
Will ye slight his grace, and die?

3 Sinners, turn, why will ye die?
God, the Spirit, asks you why!
He, who all your lives hath strove,
Woo'd you to embrace his love,
Will ye not his grace receive?
Will ye still refuse to live?
Why, ye long-sought sinners, why
Will ye grieve your God, and die?

22   **L. M.**

The Gospel Supper.

SINNERS, obey the gospel word!
  Haste to the supper of my Lord;
Be wise to know your gracious day;
All things are ready; come away!

2 Ready the Father is to own,
And kiss his late-returning son;
Ready your loving Saviour stands,
And spreads for you his bleeding hands.

3 Ready the Spirit of his love
Just now your hardness to remove;
T' apply and witness with the blood,
And wash and seal the sons of God.

4 Ready for you the angels wait,
To triumph in your bless'd estate:
Tuning their harps, they long to praise
The wonders of redeeming grace.

5 The Father, Son, and Holy Ghost,
Are ready with the shining host:
All heaven is ready to resound,
"The dead's alive! the lost is found!"

23   **L. M.**

The hearty Welcome.

COME, sinners, to the gospel feast;
  Let every scul be Jesus' guest;
Ye need not one be left behind,
For Christ hath bidden all mankind.

2 Sent by my Lord, on you I call;
The invitation is to all:
Come, all the world! come, sinner, thou!
All things in Christ are ready now.

3 Come, all ye souls by sin oppress'd,
Ye restless wand'rers after rest,
Ye poor, and maim'd, and halt, and blind,
In Christ a hearty welcome find.

4 My message as from God receive:
Ye all may come to Christ and live:
O let his love your hearts constrain,
Nor suffer him to die in vain!

5 See him set forth before your eyes,
That precious, bleeding sacrifice!
His offer'd benefits embrace,
And freely now be saved by grace.

24   8s, 7s, & 4s.

The Invitation.

COME, ye sinners, poor and needy,
  Weak and wounded, sick and sore,
Jesus ready stands to save you,
  Full of pity, love, and power;
    He is able,
He is willing, doubt no more.

2 Now, ye needy, come and welcome,
  God's free bounty glorify;
True belief and true repentance,
  Every grace that brings you nigh,
    Without money,
Come to Jesus Christ and buy.

3 Let not conscience make you linger;
　Nor of fitness fondly dream:
All the fitness he requireth
　Is to feel your need of him;
　　This he gives you,
　'Tis the Spirit's glimm'ring beam.

4 Come, ye weary, heavy-laden,
　Bruised and mangled by the fall,
If you tarry till you're better,
　You will never come at all;
　　Not the righteous,
　Sinners, Jesus came to call.

5 Agonizing in the garden,
　Lo! your Maker prostrate lies!
On the bloody tree behold him!
　Hear him cry before he dies,
　　"It is finish'd!"
　Sinners, will not this suffice?

6 Lo! th' incarnate God ascending,
　Pleads the merit of his blood;
Venture on him, venture freely;
　Let no other trust intrude:
　　None but Jesus
　Can do helpless sinners good.

7 Saints and angels, join'd in concert,
　Sing the praises of the Lamb,
While the blissful seats of heaven
　Sweetly echo with his name:
　　Hallelujah!
　Sinners here may do the same.

5 .S. M.

Praying for Repentance.

O THAT I could repent,
    With all my idols part;
And to thy gracious eye present
    An humble, contrite heart:

2 A heart with grief oppress'd
    For having grieved my God;
A troubled heart that cannot rest
    Till sprinkled with thy blood.

3 Jesus, on me bestow
    The penitent desire;
With true sincerity of wo
    My aching breast inspire:

4 With soft'ning pity look,
    And melt my hardness down:
Strike with thy love's resistless stroke,
    And break this heart of stone!

6 L. M.

Psalm li. 1-4.

SHOW pity, Lord, O Lord, forgive,
    Let a repenting rebel live;
Are not thy mercies large and free?
May not a sinner trust in thee?

2 My crimes are great, but don't surpass
The power and glory of thy grace;
Great God, thy nature hath no bound,
So let thy pard'ning love be found.

3 O wash my soul from every sin!
And make my guilty conscience clean!
Here on my heart the burden lies,
And past offences pain mine eyes.

4 My lips with shame my sins confess,
Against thy law, against thy grace;
Lord, should thy judgments grow severe,
I am condemn'd but thou art clear.

5 Should sudden vengeance seize my breath,
I must pronounce thee just in death;
And if my soul were sent to hell,
Thy righteous law approves it well.

6 Yet save a trembling sinner, Lord,
Whose hope, still hov'ring round thy word,
Would light on some sweet promise there,
Some sure support against despair.

27 S. M.

Surrendering the heart.

AND can I yet delay
My little all to give?
To tear my soul from earth away
For Jesus to receive?

2 Nay, but I yield, I yield!
I can hold out no more;
I sink, by dying love compell'd,
And own thee conqueror!

3 Though late, I all forsake;
My friends, my all resign:
Gracious Redeemer, take, O take,
And seal me ever thine!

4 Come, and possess me whole,
  Nor hence again remove:
Settle and fix my wav'ring soul
  With all thy weight of love.

·5 My one desire be this,
  Thy only love to know:
To seek and taste no other bliss,
  No other good below.

6 My life, my portion thou,
  Thou all-sufficient art:
My hope, my heavenly treasure, now
  Enter and keep my heart.

28   C. M.

Praying for faith.

FATHER, I stretch my hands to thee,
  No other help I know;
If thou withdraw thyself from me,
  Ah! whither shall I go?

2 What did thine only Son endure,
  Before I drew my breath!
What pain, what labour, to secure
  My soul from endless death!

3 O Jesus, could I this believe,
  I now should feel thy power!
Now my poor soul thou wouldst retrieve,
  Nor let me wait one hour.

4 Author of faith, to thee I lift
  My weary, longing eyes;
O let me now receive that gift,
  My soul without it dies!

5 Surely thou canst not let me die:
   O speak, and I shall live;
And here I will unwearied lie,
   Till thou thy Spirit give.

6 The worst of sinners would rejoice,
   Could they but see thy face:
O let me hear thy quick'ning voice,
   And taste thy pard'ning grace!

29   C. M.

Surrendering at the Cross.

ALAS! and did my Saviour bleed?
   And did my Sovereign die?
Would he devote that sacred head
   For such a worm as I?

2 Was it for crimes that I have done
   He groan'd upon the tree?
Amazing pity! grace unknown!
   And love beyond degree!

3 Well might the sun in darkness hide,
   And shut his glories in;
When Christ, the mighty Maker, died
   For man, the creature's sin!

4 Thus might I hide my blushing face,
   While his dear cross appears;
Dissolve my heart in thankfulness,
   And melt mine eyes to tears.

5 But drops of grief can ne'er repay
   The debt of love I owe;
Here, Lord, I give myself away,
   'Tis all that I can do.

30 **L. M.**

"I am the way."

JESUS, my all, to heaven is gone,
  He whom I fix my hopes upon;
His track I see, and I'll pursue
The narrow way, till him I view.

2 The way the holy prophets went,
The road that leads from banishment,
The King's highway of holiness,
I'll go, for all his paths are peace.

3 This is the way I long have sought,
And mourn'd because I found it not;
My grief a burden long has been,
Because I was not saved from sin.

4 The more I strove against its power,
I felt its weight and guilt the more;
Till late I heard my Saviour say,
"Come hither, soul, I AM THE WAY."

5 Lo! glad I come, and thou, bless'd Lamb,
Shalt take me to thee as I am;
Nothing but sin have I to give,
Nothing but love shall I receive.

6 Then will I tell to sinners round
What a dear Saviour I have found;
I'll point to thy redeeming blood,
And say, "Behold the way to God!"

31   **7s.**

Refuge in Christ.

JESUS, lover of my soul,
  Let me to thy bosom fly,
While the nearer waters roll,
  While the tempest still is high;
Hide me, O my Saviour, hide,
  Till the storm of life be past;
Safe into the haven guide,
  O receive my soul at last!

2 Other refuge have I none,
  Hangs my helpless soul on thee;
Leave, ah! leave me not alone,
  Still support and comfort me!
All my trust on thee is stay'd,
  All my help from thee I bring,
Cover my defenceless head
  With the shadow of thy wing.

3 Thou, O Christ, art all I want;
  More than all in thee I find:
Raise the fallen, cheer the faint,
  Heal the sick, and lead the blind.
Just and holy is thy name;
  I am all unrighteousness;
False, and full of sin, I am,
  Thou art full of truth and grace.

4 Plenteous grace with thee is found,
  Grace to cover all my sin:
Let the healing streams abound,
  Make and keep me pure within:

Thou of life the fountain art;
　Freely let me take of thee:
Spring thou up within my heart,
　Rise to all eternity!

32　　　　C. M.

The backslider's prayer.

O FOR a closer walk with God,
　　A calm and heavenly frame;
A light to shine upon the road
　That leads me to the Lamb.

2 Where is the blessedness I knew
　　When first I saw the Lord?
Where is the soul-refreshing view
　Of Jesus and his word?

3 What peaceful hours I once enjoy'd!
　　How sweet their mem'ry still!
But they have left an aching void
　The world can never fill.

4 Return, O holy Dove, return,
　　Sweet messenger of rest!
I hate the sins that made thee mourn,
　And drove thee from my breast.

5 The dearest idol I have known,
　　Whate'er that idol be,
Help me to tear it from thy throne,
　And worship only thee.

6 So shall my walk be close with God,
　　Calm and serene my frame;
So purer light shall mark the road
　That leads me to the Lamb.

33   Four 6s & two 8s.

"Whereby we cry, Abba, Father."

ARISE, my soul, arise,
  Shake off thy guilty fears,
The bleeding sacrifice
  In my behalf appears;
Before the throne my Surety stands,
My name is written on his hands.

2 He ever lives above,
  For me to intercede;
His all-redeeming love,
  His precious blood, to plead:
His blood atoned for all our race,
And sprinkles now the throne of grace.

3 Five bleeding wounds he bears,
  Received on Calvary;
They pour effectual prayers,
  They strongly speak for me:
"Forgive him, O forgive," they cry,
"Nor let that ransom'd sinner die!"

4 The Father hears him pray,
  His dear Anointed One:
He cannot turn away
  The presence of his Son:
His Spirit answers to the blood,
And tells me I am born of God.

5 My God is reconciled,
  His pard'ning voice I hear:
He owns me for his child,
  I can no longer fear:
With confidence I now draw nigh,
And Father, Abba, Father, cry.

34

C. M.

God the source of joy.

MY God, the spring of all my joys,
  The life of my delights,
The glory of my brightest days,
  And comfort of my nights!—

2 In darkest shades if thou appear,
  My dawning is begun;
Thou art my soul's bright morning star,
  And thou my rising sun.

3 The opening heavens around me shine
  With beams of sacred bliss,
If Jesus show his mercy mine,
  And whisper I am his.

4 My soul would leave this heavy clay,
  At that transporting word,
Run up with joy the shining way,
  To see and praise my Lord.

5 Fearless of hell and ghastly death,
  I'd break through every foe:
The wings of love and arms of faith
  Would bear me conqu'ror through.

35

C. M.

"His blood avail'd for me."

O FOR a thousand tongues to sing
  My great Redeemer's praise!
The glories of my God and King,
  The triumphs of his grace!

2 My gracious Master and my God,
    Assist me to proclaim,—
To spread through all the earth abroad
    The honours of thy Name.

3 Jesus! the Name that charms our fears,
    That bids our sorrows cease;
'Tis music in the sinner's ears,
    'Tis life, and health, and peace.

4 He breaks the power of cancell'd sin,
    He sets the pris'ner free:
His blood can make the foulest clean;
    His blood avail'd for *me*.

5 He speaks—and, listening to his voice,
    New life the dead receive;
The mournful, broken hearts rejoice;
    The humble poor believe.

6 Hear him, ye deaf; his praise, ye dumb,
    Your loosen'd tongues employ;
Ye blind, behold your Saviour come,
    And leap, ye lame, for joy.

36   **S. M.**
Witness of adoption.

HOW can a sinner know
    His sins on earth forgiven?
How can my gracious Saviour show
    My name inscribed in heaven?

2 What we have felt and seen
    With confidence we tell;
And publish to the sons of men
    The signs infallible.

3 We who in Christ believe
  That he for us hath died,
We all his unknown peace receive,
  And feel his blood applied.

4 Exults our rising soul,
  Disburden'd of her load,
And swells unutterably full
  Of glory and of God.

5 His love, surpassing far
  The love of all beneath,
We find within our hearts, and dare
  The pointless darts of death.

6 Stronger than death or hell
  The sacred power we prove:
And conqu'rors of the world, we dwell
  In heaven, who dwell in love.

37   **11s & 9s.**

Ecstacy of the new-born soul.

HOW happy are they Who their Saviour obey
  And have laid up their treasures above!
Tongue cannot express The sweet comfort and
    peace
  Of a soul in its earliest love!

2 That comfort was mine, When the favour
    divine
  I first found in the blood of the Lamb:
When my heart it believed, What a joy I re-
    ceived,
  What a heaven in Jesus's name!

3 'Twas a heaven below My Redeemer to know,
   And the angels could do nothing more,
Than fall at his feet, And the story repeat,
   And the Lover of sinners adore.

4 Jesus all the day long Was my joy and my
      song:
   O that all his salvation might see!
He hath loved me, I cried, He hath suffer'd
     and died,
   To redeem a poor rebel like me.

5 On the wings of his love I was carried above
   All sin, and temptation, and pain;
I could not believe That I ever should grieve,
   That I ever should suffer again.

6 I rode on the sky, Freely justified I,
   Nor did envy Elijah his seat;
My soul mounted higher In a chariot of fire,
   And the moon it was under my feet.

7 O the rapturous height Of that holy delight,
   Which I felt in the life-giving blood!
Of my Saviour possess'd, I was perfectly blest
   As if fill'd with the fulness of God.

38   **C. M.**

Perfect purification.

FOR ever here my rest shall be,
   Close to thy bleeding side:
This all my hope, and all my plea,
   For me the Saviour died.

2 My dying Saviour, and my God,
  Fountain for guilt and sin..
Sprinkle me ever with thy blood,
  And cleanse and keep me clean,

3 Wash me, and make me thus thine own;
  Wash me, and mine thou art;
Wash me, but not my feet alone,
  My hands, my head, my heart.

4 Th' atonement of thy blood apply;
  Till faith to sight improve,
Till hope in full fruition die,
  And all my soul be love.

39   C. M.

Praying for a holy heart.

O FOR a heart to praise my God,
  A heart from sin set free!
A heart that always feels thy blood
  So freely spilt for me!—

2 A heart resign'd, submissive, meek,
  My great Redcemer's throne,—
Where only Christ is heard to speak,
  Where Jesus reigns alone.

3 O for a lowly, contrite heart,
  Believing, true, and clean!
Which neither life nor death can part
  From Him that dwells within:

4 A heart in every thought renew'd
  And full of love divine;
Perfect, and right, and pure, and good,—
  A copy, Lord, of thine.
  2

40

C. M.

Psalm lxxi. 15.

MY Saviour, my almighty Friend,
  When I begin thy praise,
Where will the growing numbers end,
  The numbers of thy grace?

2 Thou art my everlasting trust;
  Thy goodness I adore:
Send down thy grace, O blessed Lord,
  That I may love thee more.

3 My feet shall travel all the length
  Of the celestial road;
And march with courage in thy strength,
  To see the Lord my God.

4 Awake! awake! my tuneful powers,
  With this delightful song,
And entertain the darkest hours,
  Nor think the season long.

41

7s.

The pilgrim's song.

CHILDREN of the heavenly King,
  As we journey let us sing;
Sing our Saviour's worthy praise,
Glorious in his works and ways.

2 We are trav'ling home to God,
In the way our fathers trod;
They are happy now, and we
Soon their happiness shall see.

3 O ye banish'd seed, be glad!
Christ our Advocate is made:
Us to save, our flesh assumes,
Brother to our souls becomes.

4 Fear not, brethren, joyful stand
On the borders of our land;
Jesus Christ, our Father's Son,
Bids us undismay'd go on.

5 Lord! obediently we'll go,
Gladly leaving all below:
Only thou our leader be,
And we still will follow thee.

42   **L. M.**

Seeking perfect rest in Christ.

O THAT my load of sin were gone!
  O that I could at last submit
At Jesus' feet to lay it down!
  To lay my soul at Jesus' feet!

2 Rest for my soul I long to find:
  Saviour of all, if mine thou art,
Give me thy meek and lowly mind,
  And stamp thine image on my heart.

3 Break off the yoke of inbred sin,
  And fully set my spirit free;
I cannot rest till pure within,
  Till I am wholly lost in thee.

4 Fain would I learn of thee, my God,
  Thy light and easy burden prove,
The cross, all stain'd with hallow'd blood,
  The labour of thy dying love.

5 I would, but thou must give the power:
    My heart from every sin release;
Bring near, bring near the joyful hour,
    And fill me with thy perfect peace.

6 Come, Lord, the drooping sinner cheer,
    Nor let thy chariot wheels delay:
Appear, in my poor heart appear!
    My God, my Saviour, come away!

43 L. M.

Apostasy deprecated.

AH! Lord, with trembling I confess,
    A gracious soul may fall from grace;
The salt may lose its seas'ning power,
And never, never find it more!

2 Lest that my fearful case should be,
Each moment knit my soul to thee;
And lead me to the mount above,
Through the low vale of humble love.

44 S. M.

Keeping the charge of the Lord.

A CHARGE to keep I have,
    A God to glorify;
A never-dying soul to save,
    And fit it for the sky:
To serve the present age,
    My calling to fulfil;—
O may it all my powers engage,
    To do my Master's will!

2 Arm me with jealous care,
  As in thy sight to live;
And, O thy servant, Lord, prepare,
  A strict account to give!
Help me to watch and pray,
  And on thyself rely,
Assured. if I my trust betray,
  I shall for ever die.

45   8s.

Delight in Christ.

HOW tedious and tasteless the hours
  When Jesus no longer I see!
Sweet prospects, sweet birds, and sweet flowers,
  Have all lost their sweetness to me,—
The midsummer sun shines but dim,
  The fields strive in vain to look gay;
But when I am happy in him,
  December's as pleasant as May.

2 His name yields the richest perfume,
  And sweeter than music his voice;
His presence disperses my gloom,
  And makes all within me rejoice;
I should, were he always thus nigh,
  Have nothing to wish or to fear,
No mortal so happy as I,
  My summer would last all the year.

3 Content with beholding his face,
  My all to his pleasure resign'd;
No changes of season or place
  Would make any change in my mind:

While bless'd with a sense of his love,
  A palace a toy would appear;
And prisons would palaces prove,
  If Jesus would dwell with me there.

4 Dear Lord, if indeed I am thine,
  If thou art my sun and my song,
Say why do I languish and pine?
  And why are my winters so long?
O drive these dark clouds from my sky,
  Thy soul-cheering presence restore;
Or take me to thee up on high,
  Where winter and clouds are no more.

46 S. M.

Rejoicing in God.

COME, ye that love the Lord,
  And let your joys be known:
Join in a song with sweet accord,
  While ye surround his throne.

2 The sorrows of the mind
  Be banish'd from the place!
Religion never was design'd
  To make our pleasures less.

3 Let those refuse to sing
  Who never knew our God;
But servants of the heavenly King
  May speak their joys abroad.

4 The God that rules on high,
  That all the earth surveys,
That rides upon the stormy sky,
  And calms the roaring seas;

5 This awful God is ours,
 Our Father and our Love;
He will send down his heavenly powers,
 To carry us above.

6 There we shall see his face,
 And never, never sin;
There, from the rivers of his grace,
 Drink endless pleasures in.

7 Then let our songs abound,
 And every tear be dry;
We're marching thro' Immanuel's ground
 To fairer worlds on high.

47   8s & 7s.

Gratitude.

COME, thou Fount of every blessing,
 Tune my heart to sing thy grace:
Streams of mercy, never ceasing,
 Call for songs of loudest praise.
Teach me some melodious sonnet,
 Sung by flaming tongues above:
Praise the mount—I'm fix'd upon it;
 Mount of thy redeeming love!

2 Here I'll raise mine Ebenezer,
 Hither, by thy help, I'm come;
And I hope, by thy good pleasure,
 Safely to arrive at home.
Jesus sought me, when a stranger,
 Wand'ring from the fold of God;
He, to rescue me from danger,
 Interposed his precious blood!

3 O! to grace how great a debtor
　　Daily I'm constrain'd to be!
Let thy goodness, like a fetter,
　　Bind my wand'ring heart to thee!
Prone to wander, Lord. I feel it;
　　Prone to leave the God I love—
Here's my heart. O take and seal it!
　　Seal it for thy courts above.

48　　　　　 ⌐C. M.
Inspiring hope.

WHEN I can read my title clear
　　To mansions in the skies,
I'll bid farewell to every fear,
　　And wipe my weeping eyes.

2 Should earth against my soul engage,
　　And fiery darts be hurl'd,
Then I can smile at Satan's rage,
　　And face a frowning world.

3 Let cares, like a wild deluge, come,
　　Let storms of sorrow fall;
So I but safely reach my home,
　　My God, my heaven, my all.

4 There I shall bathe my weary soul
　　In seas of heavenly rest,
And not a wave of trouble roll
　　Across my peaceful breast.

49　　　　　 C. M.
The heavenly Canaan.

ON Jordan's stormy banks I stand,
　　And cast a wishful eye
To Canaan's fair and happy land,
　　Where my possessions lie.

2 O the transporting, rapt'rous scene,
  That rises to my sight!
Sweet fields array'd in living green,
  And rivers of delight!

3 There gen'rous fruits that never fail,
  On trees immortal grow :
There rocks, and hills. and brooks, and vales,
  With milk and honey flow.

4 All o'er those wide-extended plains
  Shines one eternal day ;
There God the Son forever reigns,
  And scatters night away.

5 No chilling winds nor pois'nous breath
  Can reach that healthful shore;
Sickness and sorrow, pain and death,
  Are felt and fear'd no more.

6 When shall I reach that happy place,
  And be forever blest?
When shall I see my Father's face,
  And in his bosom rest?

7 Fill'd with delight, my raptured soul
  Would here no longer stay !
Though Jordan's waves around me roll,
  Fearless I'd launch away.

50   8s & 6s.

Just as I am.

JUST as I am—without one plea,
  But that thy blood was shed for me,
And that thou bidd'st me come to thee,
  O Lamb of God, I come!

Just as I am—and waiting not
To rid my soul of one dark blot,
To thee, whose blood can cleanse each spot,
    O Lamb of God, I come!

3 Just as I am—though tossed about
With many a conflict, many a doubt,
With fears within, and wars without,
    O Lamb of God, I come!

4 Just as I am, poor, wretched, blind—
Sight, riches, healing of the mind,
Yea, all I need in thee to find,
    O Lamb of God, I come!

5 Just as I am, thou wilt receive,
Wilt welcome, pardon, cleanse, relieve,
Because thy promise, I believe,
    O Lamb of God, I come!

6 Just as I am, thy love. unknown,
Has broken every barrier down;
Now to be thine, yea, thine alone,
    O Lamb of God, I come!

51   C. M.

My Mother's Bible.

THIS book is all that's left me now:
    Tears will unbidden start—
With faltering lip and throbbing brow
    I press it to my heart.
For many generations past,
    Here is our family tree;
My mother's hands this Bible clasp'd—
    She, dying, gave it me.

2 Ah! well do I remember those
　Whose names these records bear—
Who round the hearth-stone used to close
　After the evening prayer,
And speak of what these pages said—
　In tones my heart would thrill:
Though they are with the silent dead,
　Here they are living still.

3 My father read this holy book
　To brothers, sisters dear :
How calm was my poor mother's look,
　Who lean'd God's word to hear.
Her angel face—I see it yet !
　What thronging memories come !
Again that little group is met
　Within the halls of home.

4 Thou truest friend man ever knew,
　Thy constancy I've tried;
Where all were false I've found thee true—
　My counsellor and guide!
The mines of earth no treasures give
　That could this volume buy;
In teaching me the way to live,
　It taught me how to die.

52　　　　　　**7s.**

When shall we all meet again?

WHEN shall we all meet again ?
　　When shall we all meet again ?
Oft shall glowing hope aspire,
Oft shall wearied love retire,
Oft shall death and sorrow reign,
Ere we all shall meet again.

2 Though in distant lands we sigh,
Parch'd beneath the hostile sky;
Though the deep between us rolls,
Friendship shall unite our souls,
And in fancy's wide domain
There shall we all meet again.

3 When the dreams of life are fled,
When its wasted lamps are dead,
When in cold oblivion's shade
Beauty, wealth and fame are laid—
Where immortal spirits reign,
There we all may meet again.

53 6s & 5s.

When shall we meet again?—Air "UNITY."

WHEN shall we meet again?
Meet ne'er to sever?
When will peace wreathe her chain
Round us for ever?
Our hearts will ne'er repose,
Safe from the blast that blows,
In this dark vale of woes—
Never—no, never!

2 When shall love freely flow
Pure as life's river?
When shall sweet friendship glow
Changeless for ever?
Where joys celestial thrill,
Where bliss each heart shall fill,
And fears of parting chill—
Never—no, never!

3 Up to that world of light
   Take us, dear Saviour:
May we all there unite,
   Happy for ever:
Where kindred spirits dwell,
There may our music swell,
And time our joys dispel
   Never—no, never!

4 Soon shall we meet again—
   Meet ne'er to sever:
Soon will peace wreathe her chain
   Round us for ever:
Our hearts shall then repose
Secure from worldly woes;
Our songs of praise shall close
   Never—no, never!

54   11s.

Air "HOME."

MID scenes of confusion and creature com-
         plaints,
How sweet to my soul is communion with
         saints!
To find at the banquet of mercy there's room,
And feel, in the presence of Jesus, at home,
   Home, home, sweet, sweet home!
Prepare me, dear Saviour, for glory, my home.

2 While here in the valley of conflict I stay,
O give mo submission and strength as my
         day;
In all my afflictions, to thee I would come,
Rejoicing in hope of my glorious home.

·3 Whate'er thou deniest, O give me thy grace,
The Spirit's sure wituess, and smiles of thy
    face;
Let light from thy presence· disperse all my
    gloom,
And give me, e'en now, a sweet foretaste of
    home.

4 I long, gracious Lord, in thy presence to
    shine—
No more, as an exile, in sorrow to pine;
But in thy blest image arise from the tomb,
With glorified millions to praise thee at home.

55   10s & 4s.

Homeward Bound.

OUT on an ocean all boundless, we ride,
    We're homeward bound;
Tossed on the waves of a rough, restless tide,
    We're homeward bound;
Far from the safe, quiet harbor we've rode,
Seeking our Father's celestial abode,
Promise of which on us each he bestowed,
    We're homeward bound.

2 Wildly the storm sweeps us on as it roars,
    We're homeward bound;
Look! yonder lie the bright heavenly shores,
    We're homeward bound;
Steady, O pilot! stand firm at the wheel,
Steady! we soon shall outweather the gale,
O how we fly 'neath the loud creaking sail,
    We're homeward bound.

3 Down the horizon the earth disappears,
  We're homeward bound;
Joyful, O comrades! no sighing or tears,
  We're homeward bound;
Listen! what music comes soft o'er the sea!
"Welcome, thrice welcome and blessed are ye."
Can it the greeting of paradise be?
  We're homeward bound.

4 Into the harbour of heaven now we glide,
  We're home at last;
Softly we drift on its bright silver tide,
  We're home at last;
Glory to God! all our dangers are o'er;
Safely we stand on the radiant shore,
Glory to God! we will shout evermore,
  We're home at last.

56   **7s & 6s.**

Wandering Stranger.

"SAY, whither, wandering stranger,
  Ah! whither dost thou roam?
O'er this wild world a ranger,
  Hast thou no friend, no home?"
"Yes, I've a Friend who never
  Is absent from my side;
And I've a home wherever
  In peace I shall abide."

2 "But want and woe have driven
  The roses from thy cheek;
And garments rent and riven,
  Thy poverty bespeak."

"I've food with which the angels
Would all delighted be;
And robes of dazzling brightness
Are now awaiting me."

3 "Come, then, benign inquirer,
And join me on my way;
I'm journeying to a country
Where beams an endless day;
Where saints and angels, falling
Before the great white throne,
To you, to me are calling,
Haste, pilgrim, hasten home."

57   6s & 4s.

*Grateful Praises for the Gospel—Air "*AMERICA.*"*

COME, let our voices raise
A song of grateful praise,
And thankful love;
Let each a tribute bring,
Let all awake and sing
Praise to our heavenly King,
Who dwells above.

2 The gospel's sacred page,
Reveals to every age,
Salvation free.
Oh. send the joyful sound,
And let it echo round,
Till praises loud resound,
O God, to thee!

3 Accept our offerings. Lord,
To spread thy truth abroad,—
Our labors own:

At length, at thy right hand,
May we together stand,
And, with the angel-band,
Surround thy throne.

58 9s & 10s.

I'm a Pilgrim.

I'M a pilgrim, and I'm a stranger,
I can tarry, I can tarry but a night.
Do not detain me, for I am going
To where the streamlets are ever flowing—
I'm a pilgrim, and I'm a stranger,
I can tarry, I can tarry but a night.

2 There the sunbeams are ever shining,
I am longing. I am longing for the sight.
Within a country unknown and dreary,
I have been wandering forlorn and weary.
I'm a pilgrim, &c.

3 Of that country to which I'm going,
My Redeemer, my Redeemer is the light,
There are no sorrows, nor any sighing,
Nor any sin there, nor any dying,
I'm a pilgrim, &c.

59 7s & 6s.

The Happy Meeting.

HERE we suffer grief and pain,
Here we meet to part again;
In heaven we part no more.
O! that will be joyful!
When we meet to part no more.

2 All who love the Lord below,
When they die to heaven will go.
 And sing with saints above.
  O! that will be joyful!
 When we meet to part no more.

3 O! how happy we shall be!
For our Saviour we shall see,
 Exalted on his throne.
  O! that will be joyful!
 When we meet to part no more.

4 There wo all shall sing with joy,
And eternity employ
 In praising Christ, the Lord.
  O! that will be joyful!
 When we meet to part no more.

60　　　　　5s & 6s.

Heaven is my Home.

I'm but a stranger here—
 Heaven is my home;
Earth is a desert drear—
 Heaven is my home;
Dangers and sorrows stand
Round me on every hand,
Heaven is my Father-land,
 Heaven is my home.

2 What though the tempests rage,
 Heaven is my home;
Short is my pilgrimage—
 Heaven is my home;

And time's wild, wintry blast
Soon will be over past,
I shall reach home at last—
Heaven is my home.

3 Therefore I murmur not—
Heaven is my home;
What'er my earthly lot,
Heaven is my home;
And I shall surely stand
There at my Lord's right hand:
Heaven is my Father-land—
Heaven is my home.

61 7s & 6s.

Come, ere it be too late—Air " WATCHER."

O COME, in life's gay morning,
Ere in thy sunny way
The flowers of hope have withered,
And sorrow end thy day.
Come, while from joy's bright fountain
The streams of pleasure flow,
Come, ere thy buoyant spirits
Have felt the blight of woe.

2 " Remember thy Creator "
Now in thy youthful days,
And he will guide thy footsteps
Through life's uncertain maze.
"Remember thy Creator,"
He calls in tones of love,
And offers deathless glories
In brighter worlds above.

3 And in the hour of sadness,
　When earthly joys depart,
His love shall be thy solace,
　And cheer thy drooping heart.
And when life's storm is over,
　And thou from earth art free,
Thy God will be thy portion
　Throughout eternity.

62   P. M.

The Christian Soldier.

OH! when shall I see Jesus,
　And dwell with him above,
To drink the flowing fountains
　Of everlasting love?
When shall I be deliver'd
　From this vain world of sin,
And with my blessed Jesus,
　Drink endless pleasures in?

2 But now I am soldier,
　My Captain's gone before,
He's given me my orders,
　And tells me not to fear;
And if I hold out faithful,
　A crown of life he'll give,
And all his valiant soldiers
　Eternal life shall have.

3 Through grace I am determined
　To conquer though I die,.
And then away to Jesus,
　On wings of love I'll fly:

Farewell to sin and sorrow,
　I bid them all adieu ;
And you, my friends. prove faithful,
　And on your way pursue.

4 And if you meet with troubles
　And trials on the way,
Just cast your care on Jesus,
　And don't forget to pray.
Gird on the heavenly armor
　Of faith and hope and love,
And when your race is ended,
　You'll reign with him above.

5 Oh! do not be discouraged,
　For Jesus is your Friend ;
And if you lack for knowledge,
　He'll not refuse to lend :
Neither will he upbraid you,
　Though often you request,
He'll give you grace to conquer,
　And take you home to rest.

63　　　　　P. M.

Joyfully, Joyfully.

JOYFULLY, joyfully, onward I move,
　Bound for the land of bright spirits above:
Angelic choristers sing as I come,
Joyfully, joyfully haste to thy home.

2 Soon with my pilgrimage ended below,
Home to that land of delight will I go:
Pilgrim and stranger no more shall I roam ;
Joyfully, joyfully resting at home.

3 Friends, fondly cherish'd, have passed on
    before,
Waiting, they watch me approaching the
    shore;
Singing to chéer me through death's chilling
    gloom,
Joyfully, joyfully haste to thy home.

4 Sounds of sweet melody fall on my ear;
Harps of the blessed, your voices I hear!
Rings with the harmony heaven's high dome,
Joyfully, joyfully haste to thy home.

5 Death, with thy weapons of war lay me low,
Strike, king of terrors, I fear not the blow;
Jesus hath broken the bars of the tomb;
Joyfully, joyfully will I go home.

6 Bright will the morn of eternity dawn,
Death shall be banish'd, his sceptre be gone;
Joyfully then shall I witness his doom;
Joyfully, joyfully, safely at home.

64 P. L. M.

Happy Day.

PRESERVED by thine Almighty power,
    O Lord, our Maker—Saviour—King,
And brought to see this happy hour,
    We come thy praises here to sing.
     Happy day, happy day,
     Here in thy courts we'll gladly stay,
     And at thy footstool humbly pray
     That thou wouldst take our sins away.
     Happy day, happy day,
     When Christ shall wash our sins away.

2 We praise thee for thy constant care,
  For life preserved, for mercies given,
Oh, may we still those mercies share,
  And taste the joys of sins forgiven.
    Happy day, &c.

2 We praise thee for the joyful news
  Of pardon through a Saviour's blood;
Oh, Lord, incline our hearts to choose
  The path to happiness and God.
    Happy day, &c.

4 And when on earth our days are done,
  Grant, Lord, that we at length may join,
Comrades and friends around thy throne,
  The song of Moses and the Lamb.
    Happy day, &c.

65   C. M

The Shining Shore.

MY days are gliding swiftly by,
  And I, a pilgrim stranger,
Would not detain them as they fly
  Those hours of toil and danger,
For oh! we stand on Jordan's strand,
  Our friends are passing over,
And just before, the shining shore
  We may almost discover.

2 We'll gird our loins, my brethren dear,
  Our distant home discerning;
Our absent Lord has left us word,
  Let every lamp be burning,
    For oh! &c.

3 Should coming days be cold and dark,
  We need not cease our singing;
That perfect rest naught can molest,
  Where golden harps are ringing,
    For oh! &c.

  4 Let sorrow's rudest tempest blow,
    Each chord on earth to sever;
Our King says, "Come," and there's our home.
  For ever, oh! for ever!
    For oh! &c.

66   7s & 6s.

The Christian Army.

O DO not be discouraged,
  For Jesus is your Friend.
O do not be discouraged,
  For Jesus is your Friend.
He will give you grace to conquer,
He will give you grace to conquer,
  And keep you to the end.
    I am glad I'm in this army,
    Yes, I'm glad I'm in this army,
    Yes. I'm glad I'm in this army,
    And I'll battle for the truth.

  2 Fight on, ye gallant soldiers,
    The battle you shall win;
Fight on, ye gallant soldiers,
    The battle you shall win;
For the Saviour is your Captain,
For the Saviour is your Captain,
    And he has vanquished sin.
      I am glad, &c.

3 And when the conflict's over,
  Before him you you shall stand;
And when the conflict's over,
  Before him you shall stand.
You shall sing his praise for ever,
You shall sing his praise for ever,
  In Canaan's happy land.
    I am glad, &c.

67   8s & 7s.

A Home beyond the Tide.

WE are out on the ocean sailing,
  Homeward bound, we sweetly glide;
We are out on the ocean sailing,
  To a home beyond the tide,
    All the storms will soon be over,
    Then we'll anchor in the harbor;
    We are out on the ocean sailing,
    To a home beyond the tide;
    We are out on the ocean sailing,
    To a home beyond the tide.

2 Millions now are safely landed
  Over on the golden shore;
Millions more are on their journey,
  Yet there's room for millions more.
    All the storms, &c.

3 Come on board. O! "ship" for glory,
  Be in haste—make up your mind!
For our vessel's weighing anchor,
  You will soon be left behind!
    All the storms, &c.

4 You have kindred over yonder,
  On that bright and happy shore,
By-and-by we'll swell the number,
  When the toils of life are o'er.
    All the storms, &c.

5 Spread your sails, while heavenly breezes
  Gently waft, our vessel on ;
All on board are sweetly singing—
  Free salvation is the song.
    All the storms, &c.

6 When we all are safely anchored,
  We will shout—our trials o'er !
We will walk about the city,
  And we'll sing for evermore.
    All the storms, &c.

68   **P. M.**

Vain World, adieu.

WHEN for eternal worlds we steer,
  And seas are calm, and skies are clear,
And faith in lively exercise,
And distant hills of Canaan rise,
The soul for joy then claps her wings,
And loud her lovely sonnet sings,
    Vain world, adieu.

2 With cheerful hopes her eyes explore
Each landmark on the distant shore :
The trees of life, the pasture green,
The golden streets, the crystal stream ;
Again for joy she claps her wings,
And loud her lovely sonnet sings,
    Vain world, adieu.

3 The nearer still she draws to land,
More eager all her powers expand;
With steady helm and free bent sail,
Her anchor drops within the vail;
Again for joy she claps her wings,
And her celestial sonnet sings,
    Glory to God.

69   **7s.**

Watchman, what of the Night?

WATCHMAN, tell us of the night:
    What its signs of promise are.
Traveller, o'er yon mountain's height,
    See that glory-beaming star.
Watchman, does its beauteous ray
    Aught of hope or joy foretell?
Traveller, yes: it brings the day,
    Promised day of Israel.

2 Watchman tell us of the night:
    Higher yet that star ascends.
Traveller, blessedness and light,
    Peace and truth, its course portends.
Watchman, will its beams alone
    Gild the spot that gave them birth?
Traveller, ages are its own;
    See! it bursts o'er all the earth.

3 Watchman, tell us of the night,
    For the morning seems to dawn.
Traveller, darkness takes its flight,
    Doubt and terror are withdrawn.

Watchman, let thy wanderings cease:
Hie thee to thy quiet home.
Traveller, lo! the Prince of peace,
Lo! the Son of God is come.

70   8s & 3s.

Will you go.

WE'RE trav'ling home to heaven above,
        Will you go?
To sing the Saviour's dying love;
        Will you go?
Millions have reached that blest abode,
Anointed kings and priests to God,
And millions more are on the road;
        Will you go?

2 We're going to see the bleeding Lamb:
        Will you go?
In rapturous strains to praise his name;
        Will you go?
The crown of life we then shall wear,
The conqueror's palm we then shall bear,
And all the joys of heaven we'll share;
        Will you go?

3 The way to heaven is straight and plain
        Will you go?
Repent, believe. be born again;
        Will you go?
The Saviour cries aloud to thee,
"Take up thy cross and follow me,
And thou shalt my salvation see."
        Will you go?

4 We're going to join the heavenly choir,
  Will you go?
To raise our voice, and tune the lyre,
  Will you go?
There saints and angels gladly sing
Hosanna to their God and king,
And make the heavenly arches ring,
  Will you go?

71   **11s.**

" I would not live alway."

I WOULD not live alway: I ask not to stay
Where storm after storm rises dark o'er the
  way;
The few lurid mornings that dawn on us
  here,
Are enough for life's woes, full enough for its
  cheer.

2 I would not live alway: no—welcome the
  tomb,
Since Jesus hath lain there, I dread not its
  gloom;
There, sweet be my rest, till He bid me arise,
To hail him in triumph descending the skies.

3 Who, who would live alway, away from his
  God—
Away from yon heaven, that blissful abode, ·
Where the rivers of pleasure flow o'er the
  bright plains,
And the noontide of glory eternally reigns:

4 Where the saints of all ages in harmony
    meet,
Their Saviour and brethren transported to
    greet:
While the anthems of rapture unceasingly roll,
And the smile of the Lord is the feast of the
    soul!

72   L. M.

PRAISE God, from whom all blessings flow:
    Praise him, all creatures here below:
Praise him above, ye heavenly host—
Praise Father, Son and Holy Ghost.

73   C. M.

NOW let the Father, and the Son,
    And Spirit be adored
Where there are works to make him known,
    Or saints to love the Lord.

74   S. M.

GIVE to the Father praise,
    Give glory to the Son;
And to the Spirit of his grace
    Be equal honor done.

75   7s.

SING we to our God above
    Praise eternal as his love:
Praise him, all ye heavenly host—
Father, Son, and Holy Ghost.

INDEX.

The figures refer to the page.

* 9 7 8 3 3 3 7 1 3 6 7 6 5 *